DATE DUE

Honeyman, Susannah.

Saudi Arabia

Saudi Arabia

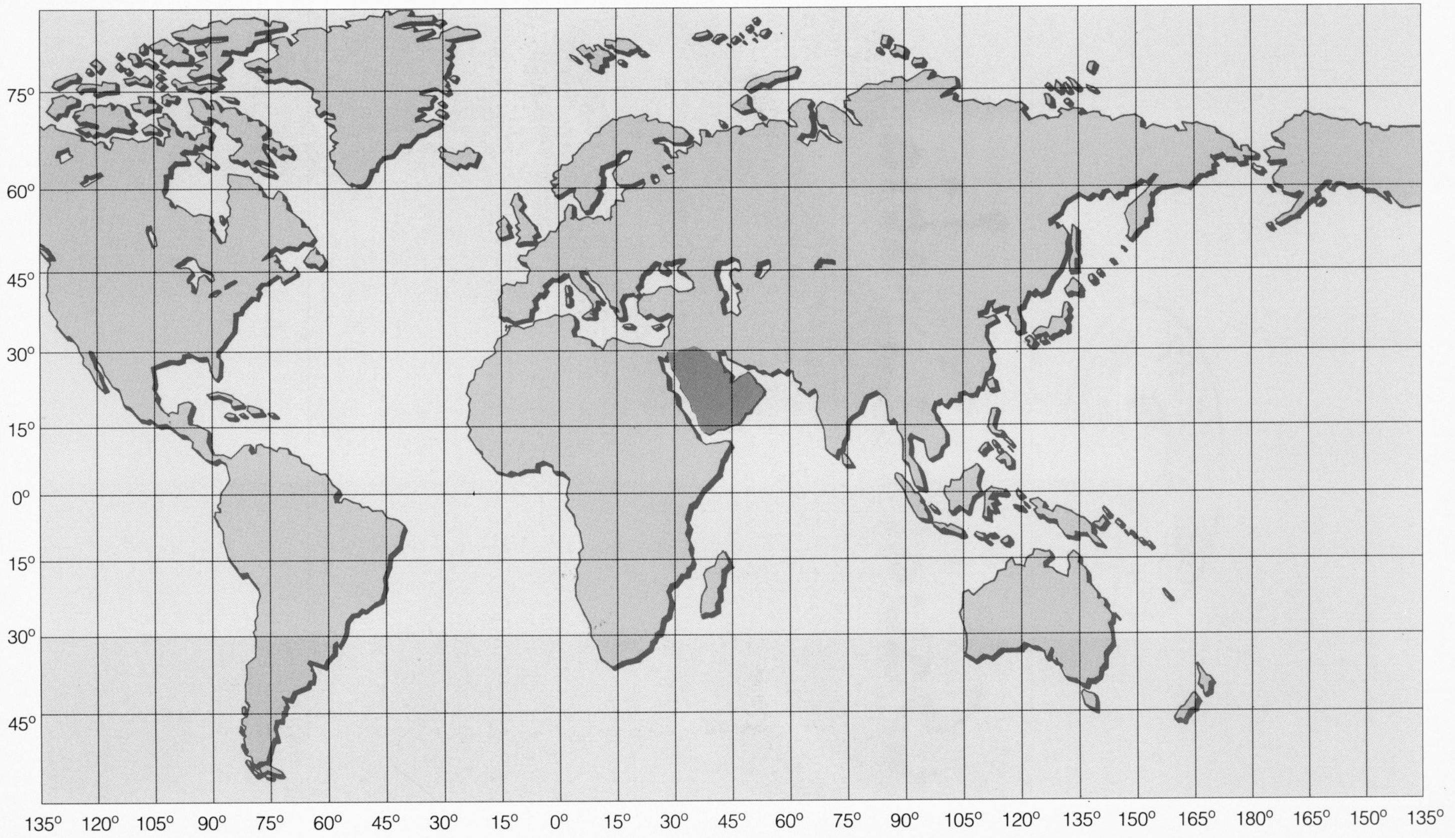
75°
60°
45°
30°
15°
0°
15°
30°
45°
135° 120° 105° 90° 75° 60° 45° 30° 15° 0° 15° 30° 45° 60° 75° 90° 105° 120° 135° 150° 165° 180° 165° 150° 135°

IRAQ
IRAN
JORDAN
KUWAIT
PERSIAN GULF
Tabuk
Ha'il
Al-Jubayl
Ras Tannurah
Al-Qatif
Ad-Dammam
Dhahran
BAHRAIN
QATAR
Al-Hufuf
Buraydah
RIYADH
STRAIT OF HORMUZ
OMAN
GULF OF OMAN
EGYPT
RED SEA
Medina
Yanbu' al-Bahr
SAUDI ARABIA
UNITED ARAB EMIRATES
Tropic of Cancer
Rabigh
Layla
Jeddah
Mecca
At-Ta'if
20°
20°
OMAN
SUDAN
N
W
E
S
Abha
Najran
Jizan
FARASAN ISLANDS
ARABIAN SEA
ERITREA
YEMEN
ETHIOPIA
BAB EL MANDEB STRAITS
DJIBOUTI
GULF OF ADEN
GULF OF AQABA
0
250 mi
500 km

Saudi Arabia

Susannah Honeyman

RAINTREE STECK-VAUGHN
PUBLISHERS

Austin, Texas

Published by Raintree Steck-Vaughn Publishers, an imprint of Steck-Vaughn Company

Design Roger Kohn
Editor Diana Russell, Helene Resky
DTP editor Helen Swansbourne
Picture research Valerie Mulcahy
Illustration János Márffy
Consultant Don Kerr
Commissioning editor Debbie Fox

We are grateful to the following for permission to reproduce photographs:
Front Cover: TRIP/Helene Rogers *above*, R. Warburton/Middle East Pictures *below;* Aspect Picture Library, pages 24 *above* (Don Smetzer), 25 and 35 *above* (Peter Carmichael); Associated Press/Topham Picture Source, page 17 *left*; J. Allan Cash Photolibrary, page 14 *below*; Robert Harding Picture Library, pages 8 *below* (Peter Ryan), 11, 13 (James Green), 18 (David Lomax), 30 (James Green), 39 *below*; Magnum, pages 19 *above* (Abbas), 26 *below* (Bruno Barbey), 40 (Abbas); The Military Picture Library, page 28 (Geoff Lee); Christine Osborne/Middle East Pictures, pages 10, 31 *above*; Oxford Scientific Films, page 38 (Eyal Bartov); Picturepoint, pages 16 (Tomkinson), 23, 24, *below*, 33 *above*; Peter Sanders Photography, pages 12–13, 14–15, 22 *above*, 31 *below*, 34 *below*; Frank Spooner Pictures/Gamma, pages 8 *above*, 20 and 26 *above* (Halstead), 27 (D. E. Keerle), 42 (Laurent van der Stockt); Tony Stone Images, pages 9, 32; Sygma, page 37 (J. Langevin); TRIP/Helene Rogers, pages 12, 17 *right*, 19 *below*, 21, 22 *below*, 29, 33 *below*, 34 *above*, 35 *below*, 36, 39 *above;* R. Warburton/Middle East Pictures, page 41

Grateful thanks to the Meteorological Office, Bracknell, for supplying information for the chart on page 15

The statistics given in this book are the most up-to-date available at the time of going to press.

Printed and bound in Hong Kong by Paramount Printing Group

2 3 4 5 6 7 8 9 0 HK 99 98 97 96

Library of Congress Cataloging-in-Publication Data
Honeyman, Susannah.
Saudi Arabia / Susannah Honeyman.
p. cm. – (Country fact files)
Includes index.
ISBN 0-8114-2786-2
1. Saudi Arabia – Juvenile literature. [1. Saudi Arabia.]
I. Series.
DS204.H65 1995
953–dc20
94-17104
CIP AC

CONTENTS

Words that are explained in the glossary are printed in SMALL CAPITALS the first time they are mentioned in the text.

INTRODUCTION

The kingdom of Saudi Arabia was created more than 60 years ago, in 1932. The people of this ancient homeland of the Arabs were mainly poor farmers and NOMADIC herders, who struggled to make a living among the hottest deserts on Earth. Some merchants in the towns traded with East Africa, Persia (Iran), and India in small wooden ships, just as their ancestors had done in the Middle Ages.

Today Saudi Arabia is one of the richest and most powerful countries in the world. In the 1930s American prospectors discovered oil in the country. Saudi Arabia has the world's biggest oil reserves and is the world's biggest exporter of oil. Since the 1960s, Saudi Arabia has earned billions of dollars from its oil and has used its wealth to build modern cities, services, and strong armed forces.

But Saudi Arabia is also powerful for another reason. Islam was founded there in the 7th century A.D. and soon spread through northern Africa, the Middle East, and Asia. Now one-seventh of the world's population is Muslim, and Saudi Arabia is their holy land. Every day almost a billion people in more than 70 countries face in the direction of Mecca, in Saudi Arabia, to pray. And every year up to 2 million Muslims travel to Saudi Arabia on a PILGRIMAGE to the most sacred places of Islam.

Wealth has changed the life-style of most Saudi people, through education, health care, modern housing, and transportation. But everyday life in Saudi Arabia is still based on religious beliefs and customs that are stricter than in almost any other Muslim country, except Iran. Traditional ways and advanced technology exist side by side.

All over the world people depend on Saudi oil and gas for needs like petroleum and kerosene, electricity, plastics, medicines, fertilizer, and synthetic fibers.

These ancient rock tombs were built by the Nabateans of northwest Arabia. For 400 years, up to A.D. 105, the Nabateans controlled overland trade from Yemen, India, and Persia (Iran) to the Roman Empire.

SAUDI ARABIA AT A GLANCE

- Area: 830,000 square miles (2,150,000 sq km)
- Population (1993 estimate): 12.3 million Saudi nationals, plus 4.6 million foreign workers (total population 16.9 million)
- Population density: 19 persons per square mile (7 per sq km)
- Capital: Riyadh, population 1.7 million
- Other main cities: Jeddah 1.3 million; Mecca 463,000; Medina 260,000; At-Ta'if 250,000; ad-Dammam–Dhahran 250,000
- Highest mountain: Mount Sawda, 10,522 feet (3,207 m)
- Language: Arabic
- Religion: Islam (98% Sunni Muslims; 2% Shia Muslims)
- Literacy (1987): 52 percent
- Currency: Saudi riyal, written as SR, divided into 100 halalah
- Economy: Based on oil and gas production and exports, with developing industry, agriculture, and banking
- Major resources: Oil and gas reserves
- Major products: Crude and refined oil and gas products
- Environmental problems: Shortage of water, advancing desert, oil pollution

►***Mecca, the birthplace of the Prophet Muhammad, contains the most sacred place in Islam: the Ka'aba shrine. It is at the center of the Great*** MOSQUE, ***draped in black cloth and decorated with verses from the*** KORAN ***woven in gold. Every Muslim has a religious duty to try to make a pilgrimage to Mecca.***

THE LANDSCAPE

Saudi Arabia is a land of many kinds of deserts. There are rugged mountain ranges, "seas" of sand, rocky plains, salt flats, and plateaus with deep gorges and dry valleys. It is one of the most hostile environments on Earth for people, but it is also a land of variety, with areas of great natural beauty.

The country occupies 80 percent of the Arabian PENINSULA, which began to break away from the continent of Africa 35 million years ago. As they parted, the ocean flooded the northern Great Rift Valley to form the Red Sea.

The wedge-shaped peninsula is bordered on the west by the Red Sea and on the east by the Persian Gulf and the Arabian Sea. In the north, desert forms a natural barrier between Saudi Arabia and neighboring Jordan, Iraq, and Kuwait. There are land borders in the east with the United Arab Emirates and Qatar, while the tiny island state of Bahrain lies off the coast. In the southeast, mountains separate Saudi Arabia from Oman and Yemen.

The Hejaz Mountains run parallel to the Red Sea for 1,000 miles (1,600 km), from Medina to the Gulf of Aqaba. In the southern Hejaz the ranges reach 10,000 feet (3,000 m) and average 5,000 feet (1,500 m) at the northern end. Raised fossil coral reefs form sheer cliffs, broken by narrow inlets. Exposed coral reefs in the southern Red Sea form the Farasan Islands.

Until 600 years ago, there were active

KEY FACTS

- Arabia is moving away from Africa at the rate of 1.6 inches (4 cm) a year.
- The average depth of the Persian Gulf is only 112 feet (35 m), and its deepest point is 332 feet (100 m). The Red Sea reaches 9,350 feet (2,850 m) in depth.
- Ar-Rub' al-Khali is the largest sand desert in the world — bigger than France, Belgium, and the Netherlands combined.
- Traditional houses in Jeddah are built from ancient coral rock cut from the Red Sea coast.
- Some villages in remote valleys in the Asir can only be reached by using rope ladders.

▲The shallow waters of the Persian Gulf meet the low-lying desert plain of Eastern Province in a network of tidal creeks.

◄Ar-Rub' al-Khali. Ridges and dunes of red sand formed by fierce monsoon rains during the last Ice Age tower 1,000 feet (300 m) above white salt flats.

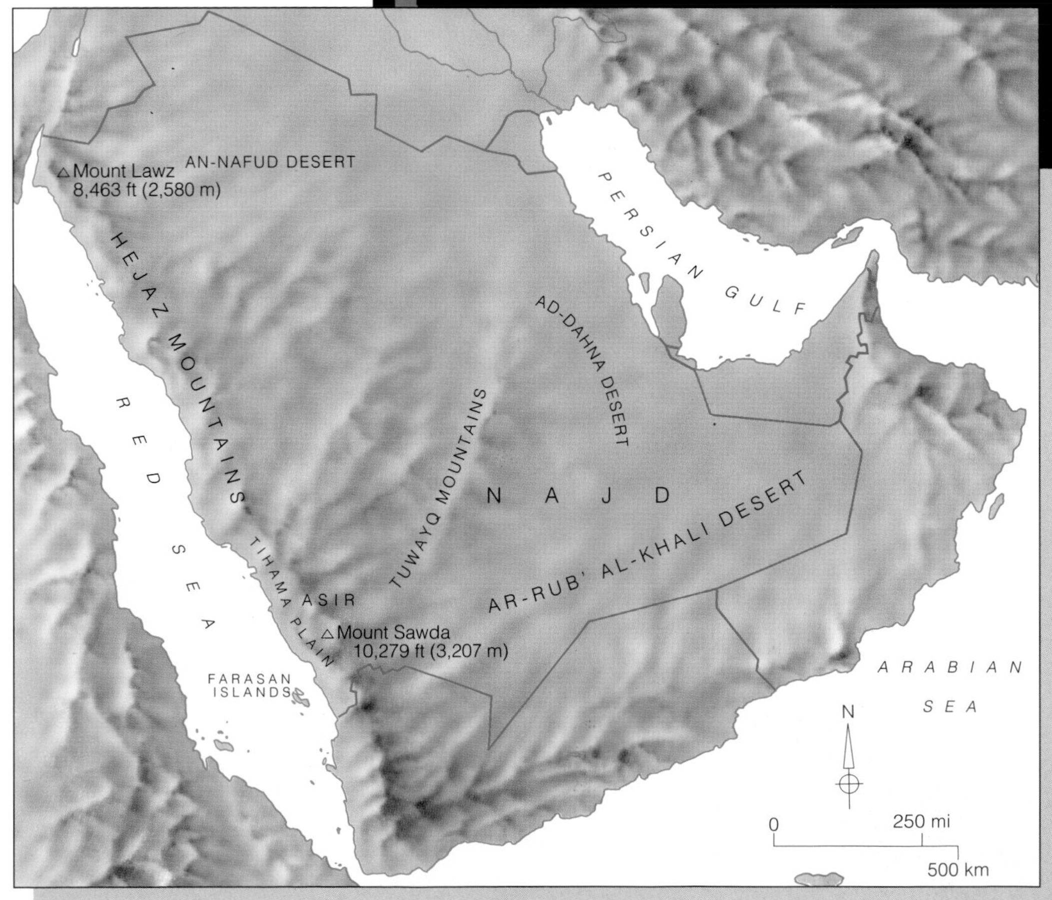

◀ ***Asir Province in the southwest has the country's highest mountains and, on the Red Sea coast, old lava flows and mangrove swamps.*** TERRACES ***on the slopes make full use of the soil and climate here, which are suited to farming.***

volcanoes in western Saudi Arabia. But all that remains today are black boulders of volcanic rock called basalt, scattered over the plains and mountain slopes.

The remote southwestern Asir region is also mountainous, averaging 5,000 feet (1,500 m) but with higher peaks, including the highest in the country, Mount Sawda 10,522 feet (3,207 m). As this region has a much higher rainfall than the rest of the country, it has denser vegetation, and during the MONSOON rains, has many seasonal rivers and waterfalls. The Tihama Plain lies between the Asir highlands and the coast.

Behind the Hejaz, to the east, lies the plateau of Najd, which is covered in deep gullies made by the wind and tropical rains. Some mountain ranges here rise to 1,650 feet (500 m) above the plateau. The Najd slopes toward low-lying plains in the east. This region was once the bed of an ancient sea, shrunk by climatic change, which survives today as the shallow Persian Gulf. Along the gulf coast there is a wide zone of salt flats, tidal marshes, and, here and there, MANGROVE swamps.

To the north and south of this eastern

plain are two of the great hot deserts of the world. In the north, the An-Nafud Desert is a flat, stony expanse covering 22,000 square miles (57,000 sq km). In southeast Saudi Arabia lies the formidable sand desert of ar-Rub' al-Khali ("the Empty Quarter"), an area of 250,970 square miles (650,000 sq km). These two deserts are linked by an 800-mile (1,300-km) arc of shifting, sandy desert called ad-Dahna.

In all of Saudi Arabia there are only two natural freshwater lakes, both at Layla in the central Tuwayq Mountains. There are no permanent rivers. Dry gullies (WADIS) channel water after rainstorms.

The most typical natural vegetation is low-growing thorn bushes and scrub. The dusty scene is varied by oases, green and fertile areas around natural springs and wells that can range in size from a few acres to many square miles. The biggest are north of Riyadh (at Ha'il and Buraydah), south of the city (al-Kharj), and in the eastern region (at Al-Hufuf and Al-Qatif). These and other oases have been developed using modern agricultural methods.

An oasis at Ha'il in the northern Najd, near the An-Nafud Desert. Dates and vegetables are grown on fertile land around permanent springs at the foot of arid mountain ranges.

Mountains of the Hejaz, near Jeddah. Black volcanic rock of hardened lava is covered with a drifting layer of sand.

CLIMATE AND WEATHER

Most of Saudi Arabia is very dry, with great extremes of temperature. The little rain that does fall is scarce and erratic.

The country lies between the weather systems of the Mediterranean and the tropics. The northwesterly winter rains from the Mediterranean affect the northern Hejaz but weaken as they cross the mountains and reach the An-Nafud Desert. At higher altitudes the winter brings frost and even snow.

At this time, too, a dry northeast wind called the SHAMAL crosses the country. The sand it carries falls as a haze of brown dust, which finds its way into every nook and cranny, indoors as well as outside.

Between May and October the winds shift to the southwest and blow strongly, carrying moist air picked up from the Indian Ocean. The greatest amount of rain falls in the high Asir, 19 inches (480 mm) a year. Farther

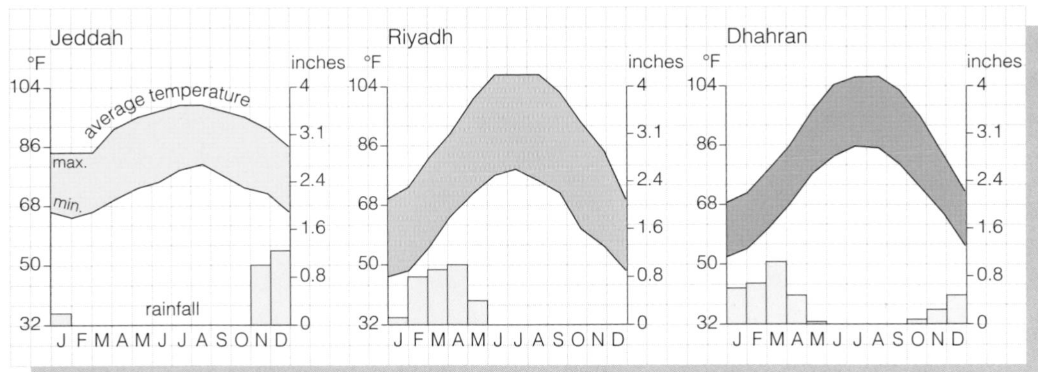

▲ ***Temperatures on the coast do not reach as high as in the interior, but at sea level the atmosphere is much more humid.***

◀ ***After a rainstorm, floods drain into a wadi, providing temporary surface water.***

◀ ***The pool of cool blue water among these dunes is not real. It is a mirage caused by extreme heat.***

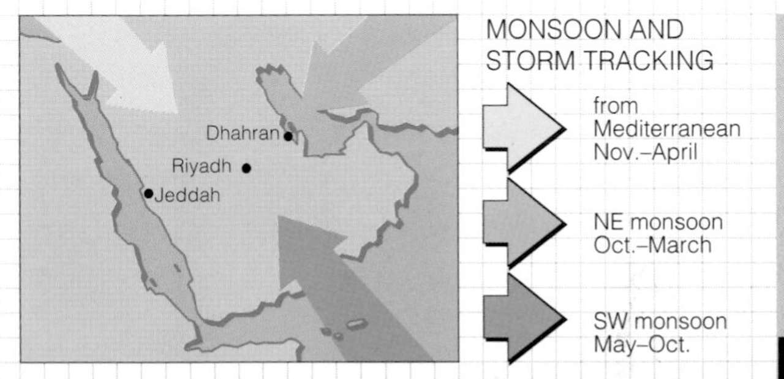

KEY FACTS

- The highest temperature recorded in Saudi Arabia is 129°F (54°C).
- The Tropic of Cancer passes through Saudi Arabia south of Medina, so the sun is directly overhead at noon on June 21.

east, these monsoon clouds evaporate as they rise over the mountains along the border with Yemen and Oman. Most of the rain they carry falls on the southern slopes of the mountains. If the monsoons do push northward, the rain comes in heavy thunderstorms, but is unreliable and, therefore, of little use to farmers. The country's average annual rainfall is 1.5–4 inches (30–100 mm), but in most areas outside Asir Province 10 or even 20 years' drought is not unusual.

The cloudless skies over central Saudi Arabia mean that there are extremes of temperature. Daytime temperatures are very high, averaging 86°F (30°C) and often reaching over 104°F (40°C) in summer, but the temperature plummets after sunset. It is not unusual to experience a range of 72°F (40°C) in one day. In the summer, Riyadh is so hot that the government moves to the cooler mountain town of At-Ta'if, in the Hejaz. But in winter, morning frost in Riyadh is common.

On the coasts humidity is higher. Even the more moderate temperatures there feel uncomfortable.

NATURAL RESOURCES

Below the deserts of Saudi Arabia lie huge reservoirs of its most precious natural resources: water and oil. Water is very scarce, because more than 90 percent of the land receives no regular rainfall. There are no permanent rivers to provide supplies of water and feed lakes.

However, since ancient times, desert people have made use of FOSSIL WATER. This forms when rain falls and filters through the ground until it is trapped by a "waterproof" layer of rock. The water then spreads out. Where the rock dips into a saucer shape, the water collects in a pool. Over thousands of years, rain falling on the Hejaz Mountains has been trapped underground in this way.

Where the water appears at the surface naturally, springs form, and oases develop. The biggest oases in Saudi Arabia are at al-Hasa and north and south of Riyadh, in Eastern Province. The largest springs appear at two lakes in Layla. Where the water is near enough to the surface, it can be reached by digging wells. These can be between 23–50 feet (7–15 m) deep if dug by hand, but with modern equipment water can be pumped from a depth of hundreds of feet.

Oil and gas, formed many millions of years ago from decaying animal and plant matter, were trapped underground in much

Drilling for oil in the desert in Eastern Province.

Saudi Arabia's climate is ideal for solar power, but so far there are only experimental projects, like the one below.

Riyadh depends on water piped from* DESALINATION *plants on the east coast. Its water tower is a landmark.

the same way as water. Saudi Arabia has the biggest oil reserves in the world. It has a fourth of the world's known reserves of over 991 billion barrels. The country's oil fields lie under the eastern plain and the Persian Gulf. This whole region is rich in oil.

Other natural resources in Saudi Arabia include large deposits of iron ore and smaller quantities of copper, gold, and zinc. However, there has been little interest in developing these, because it would not be profitable.

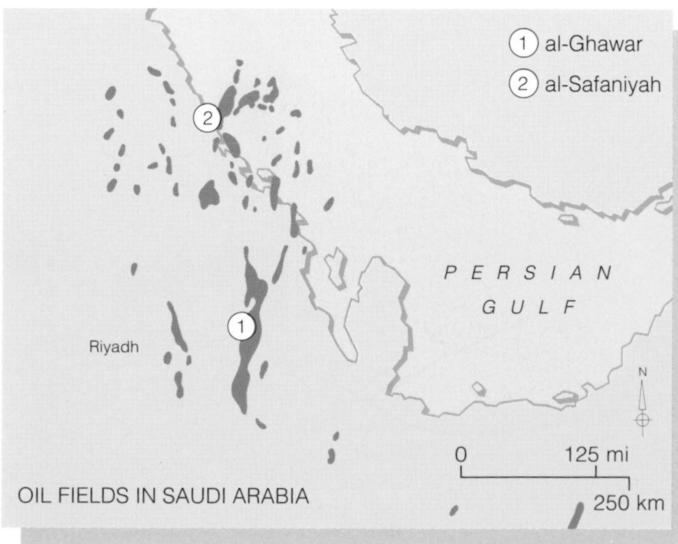

OIL FIELDS IN SAUDI ARABIA

KEY FACTS

- Fossil water used to irrigate fields at al-Hasa is 17,000 years old.
- There are freshwater springs on the bed of the Persian Gulf.
- Oil is measured in "barrels" (bbls) and production in "barrels per day" (bpd).
- There are only 37 "supergiant" oil fields in the world, each with over 5 billion barrels of oil. Saudi Arabia has 11, including the world's biggest onshore and offshore fields (al-Ghawar and al-Safaniyah).

POPULATION

The people who live in Saudi Arabia fall into two separate groups. About 12 million are Saudi nationals, and about 4.5 million are EXPATRIATES, or foreigners who are allowed to live there to work.

TRADITIONAL LIFE-STYLES

Most Saudis in the interior used to live in villages, farming at oases and in fertile wadis. Others lived as nomadic herders. The Bedouins (which means "desert dwellers") herded camels, goats, and sheep, moving their camps with the seasons to give their animals the best available feeding and water supplies. In the hottest months the Bedouins moved to the edge of the oases, where they traded their products, such as leather, for goods from the towns and villages.

In the towns, especially along the coasts, there were many prosperous merchants and craftsmen. They lived by trading with the interior, with other regions of Arabia, or even with East Africa and India.

SAUDI ARABIA TODAY

Since the 1960s, Saudis have increasingly left their traditional way of life. Now 73 percent work in the fast-growing towns and cities. They work in business, government administration, and the armed forces. Those who remain in the countryside have also changed their life-style, because they can afford radios, kerosene stoves, vehicles, and small luxuries. Today few Bedouins

◀ ***The bazaar* (SOUK) *in Jeddah is always busy. Traditional merchants' houses, four or five stories high, were built from coral rock and teak. Carved wooden screens at the window allow women to watch the street below without being seen.***

◀ ***It is a Bedouin custom to offer coffee to a guest and an insult to refuse it. In the towns, coffeehouses are a favorite place for men to sit and relax.***

▼ ***This Saudi family is strolling down a street in Jeddah. But in stricter areas, such as Riyadh, a woman could not appear in public with her face uncovered.***

KEY FACTS

- Saudi Arabia has the world's third highest population growth rate at 5.6 percent. At this rate the population will double by the year 2006.
- Riyadh has the world's highest urban expansion rate. Its population has grown 500 percent in 20 years.
- In 1992 the biggest group of pilgrims to Mecca came from Indonesia (125,000), followed by Iran (116,000) and Pakistan (87,000).

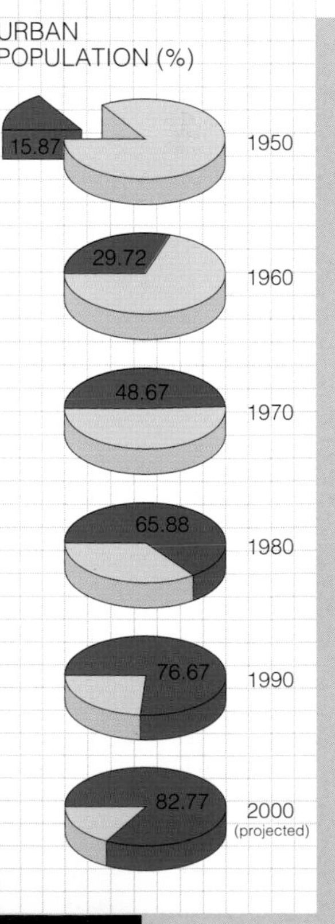

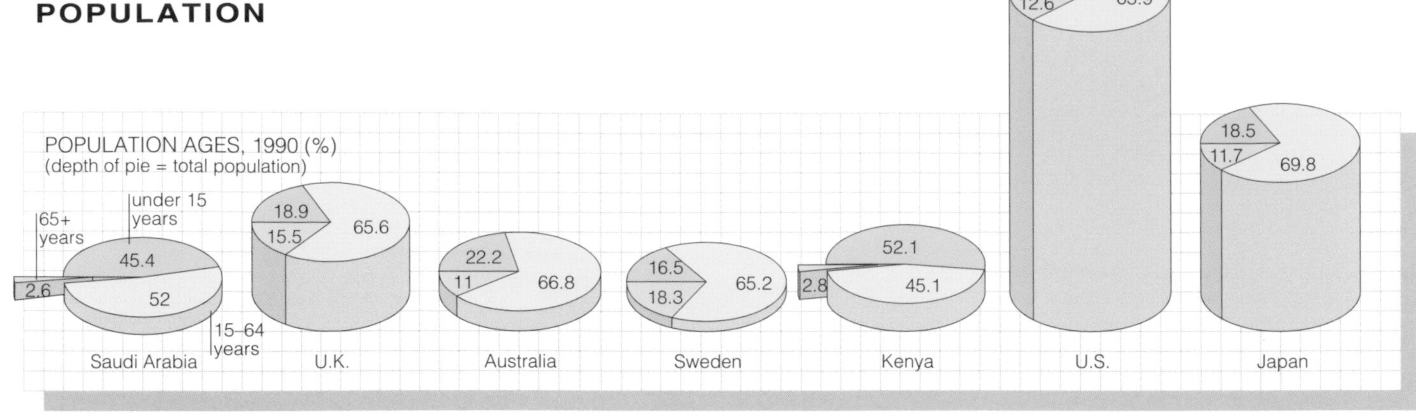

depend on a nomadic existence.

But some traditions remain very strong. People's names immediately show their tribe and family line, and there are strong regional and family loyalties. Islam and Arabic are the common bond between all Saudis.

In the remote southwestern Asir, people have distinctive traditions — different houses, clothing, and culture. Women here do not wear the veil. Their traditional dress includes wide-brimmed straw hats with high crowns.

EXPATRIATES AND PILGRIMS

Foreigners who work in Saudi Arabia are only permitted to enter the country on temporary contracts. They cannot remain

◀ ***Almost half of all Saudis are less than 15 years old.***

▶ ***Saudi Arabia's water resources are scarce, but there is no lack of land.***

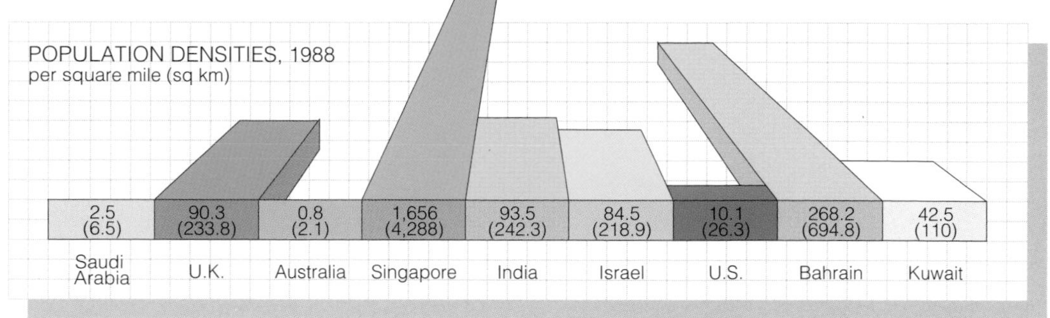

permanently. Some are highly qualified professionals, such as engineers, architects, doctors, and bankers. Many more are unskilled laborers. Expatriate workers from the Philippines alone (400,000) account for 15 percent of all domestic servants and more than 50 percent of all hospital staff in Saudi Arabia.

Each year up to 2 million Muslims of more than 70 nationalities come to Saudi Arabia on pilgrimage. For several weeks the government must provide shelter (mainly tents), water, food, and medical, transportation, and other services for pilgrims staying outside Mecca. This is the equivalent of setting up a city where no one speaks a common language.

◀ ***Thai and Filipino construction workers in Al-Jubayl. Saudi Arabia's modernization could not have been achieved without the millions of expatriates who have worked there.***

▶ ***Expatriates relax on the weekend with a barbecue around the pool in their own accommodation complex.***

DAILY LIFE

RELIGION

Islam, the religion of Saudi Arabia, has many rules for public and private behavior, as well as religious duties. All non-Muslims in the country must also follow some of these rules.

The workweek runs from Saturday morning to Thursday midday, and during the week, offices close at prayer times. Muslims obey the MUEZZIN's call to prayer five times daily: at dawn, noon, mid-afternoon, sunset, and evening. People pray in the mosque or in public places, always facing toward Mecca. The main prayer gathering is at noon on Friday, the Muslim holy day. Exact times of sunrise, sunset, and the new moon appear in Saudi newspapers.

EDUCATION

Education is an important part of Islam. Boys especially must learn the Koran, the holy book, by heart and learn the *Hadith* (traditions). They attend special schools (MADRASSA) where they are given Koranic teaching.

Schooling is free and available to everyone. Boys and girls are educated separately. When the first state girls' school opened in 1963, many people complained to the king. The first college was opened in 1958. Now renamed the University of Riyadh, it has separate men's and women's campuses, with a total of about 20,000 students. Today there are other universities and colleges, too, including the University of Petroleum and Minerals at Dhahran. Many male students seek special training overseas.

These worshipers are in the Prophet's Mosque at Medina, which is being extended to hold 257,000 people. The Great Mosque, in Mecca, holds 1 million.

HAJJ *pilgrims wear seamless white robes to hide differences in wealth or nationality. After Id al-Adha, they shave their heads as a sign of purity.*

THE ISLAMIC CALENDAR AND FESTIVALS

The Islamic calendar begins on July 16 A.D. 622, when the Prophet Muhammad left Mecca for Medina. The Islamic year has 12 lunar months, which start when the new moon appears, totaling 354 days. Each day starts at sunset precisely and runs until the next sunset. Friday is the holy day and day of rest.

The only public holidays in Saudi Arabia are religious festivals. These include 10 days at Id al-Fitr at the end of Ramadan, the month of fasting, and 4 days at Id al-Adha, the tenth day of the month of the hajj. New Year is the first of the month of Muharram.

January 1, 1994	19 Rajab 1414
June 9, 1994	1 Muharram 1415
May 30, 1995	1 Muharram 1416
May 19, 1996	1 Muharram 1417

Saudi schoolchildren are still taught by traditional methods, learning the Koran by heart. Expatriate children go to different schools.

KEY FACTS

- Correct behavior is enforced by the religious police (MUTAWA), who patrol the streets and even enter private houses to check on people.
- In 1958 Saudi Arabia had only 20 primary schools, but by 1987 it had over 10,500.
- The Arabic language is written from right to left.
- Gambling and alcohol are forbidden throughout Saudi Arabia.

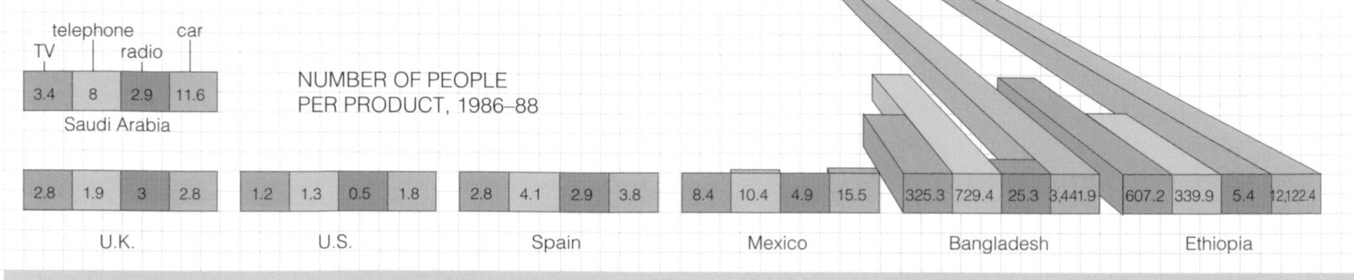

Saudis can afford to buy many imported goods.

This Saudi home is decorated with colorful carpets and local craftwork. Women live in a separate section of the house.

Jewelry in the gold souk is sold by weight, at prices that are updated daily. Sales are worth around $1.3 billion a year.

HOME LIFE

In Islam, a man may have up to four wives, so a large family of half-brothers and half-sisters and their mothers may all live in one house. At home, Saudi women and girls have separate living areas and bedrooms and do not eat with the men and boys. In the street or at work, a female must follow certain strict rules. She must not speak to a man, or even sit beside him, unless he is a member of her family. She must cover her hair, arms, and legs in public with a long cloak, though she may be wearing jeans or a designer dress underneath. Expatriate women often wear cloaks in public, too. In the strictest areas (like Riyadh) Saudi females must also cover their faces with a veil or mask.

Saudi men and boys wear simple long cotton robes and a loose headdress held in place by a black ropelike band. This national dress is the same for all, with little difference for rich and poor, although there are regional variations. It is a practical and comfortable way to dress and shield the head from the hot sun. But at home, or when overseas, men often wear the same jeans or business suits as those around them.

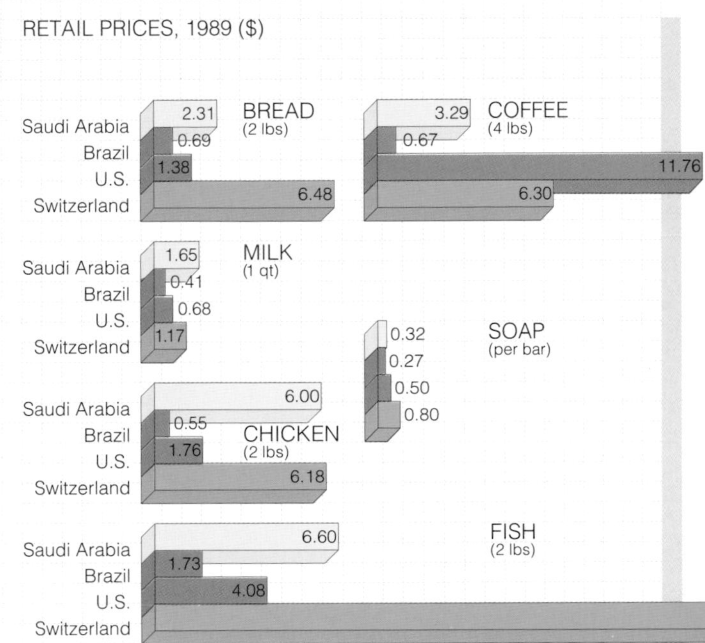

KEY FACTS

- In Islam the left hand is considered unclean, so it is never used in greeting or to pass something.
- Saudi parents arrange the marriages of their sons and daughters.
- Saudi Arabia has the highest rate of death from diabetes in the world: 60 people die from it each day.
- Saudi men and women do not usually work at the same businesses.

Saudi health services have some of the most advanced hospitals in the world, but most medical staff are foreign. King Faisal Hospital in Riyadh is one of the best hospitals in the Middle East. However, many Bedouins still use traditional medicine.

The coast road in Jeddah has been decorated with many lively sculptures. Saudi and expatriate families enjoy the beach, but Saudi women and girls do not wear swimsuits in public.

LEISURE

Traditional leisure activities include hunting with falcons or dogs, and horse and camel racing. Soccer and water sports are also popular now. People in towns enjoy picnics in the desert on weekends either just for the day or camping in Bedouin style. Films and television programs are strictly censored to conform with Islam, but Arabic music is heard everywhere in Saudi Arabia.

Islam forbids drunkenness, and all alcohol is banned in the country, so there are no clubs or bars, even in hotels. The traditional drink is coffee. There are harsh punishments for importing alcohol, drugs, and certain videos or books. The same rules apply to expatriates.

The King's Camel Race is held in April or May, near Riyadh. Thousands of camels take part in the 12-mile (19-km) race through the desert for big prize money. The jockeys are young boys who make sure they stay mounted by attaching Velcro® to the saddle!

RULES AND LAWS

Saudi Arabia is an Islamic monarchy. The ruling Saud family belongs to the strict Wahhabi branch of Islam, which was founded in Najd. The king is titled the Custodian of the Two Holy Places, because this is his greatest duty. He is also the country's IMAM, or religious leader. The traditional form of government among Bedouin Arabs is the MAJLIS, an open meeting where all subjects can plead their case. The king still holds *majlis,* as do local tribal leaders.

The country is not a democracy. There are no political parties, no one can vote, and there is no Parliament. The king (who is also prime minister) and his Council of Ministers

King Fahd is descended from Ibn Saud, who unified the kingdom in 1932.

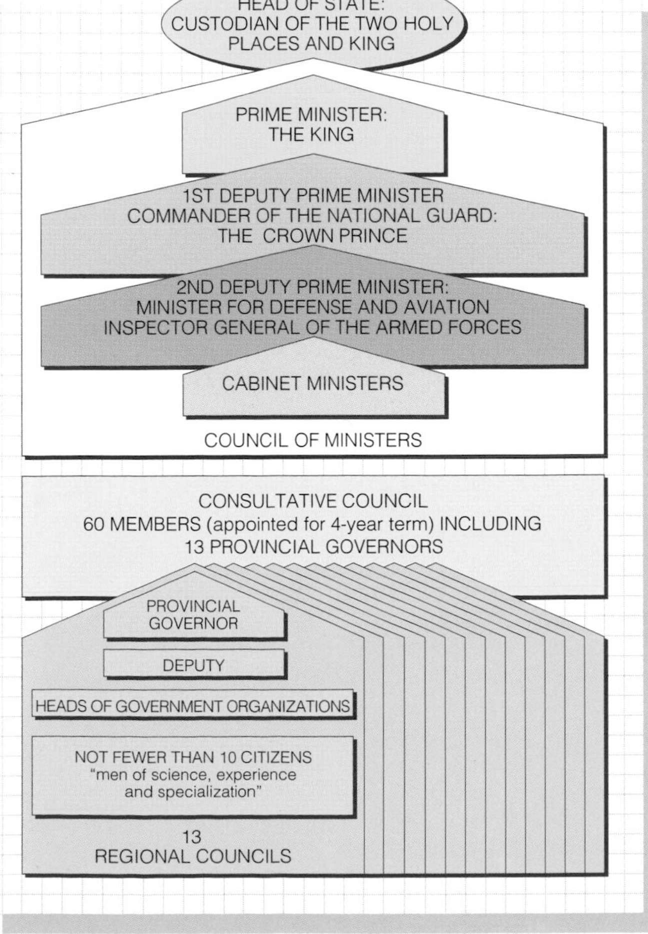

"There is no god but God; and Muhammad is His Messenger." These words from the Koran appear on the Saudi flag, together with a traditional Arabian sword.

approve all government decisions. The two deputy prime ministers (who are also members of the royal family) head the armed forces, which are among the best equipped in the Middle East.

Saudi social, political, and economic law is based on the Islamic SHARIA, and courts have religious judges (QADI). Crimes such as theft, adultery, and murder carry harsh penalties, including execution. The crime rate is low.

After the Gulf War in 1990–91, the Saudi king announced political reforms. In 1993 the 60-member Consultative Council was created to review decisions made by the government.

In August 1990 Iraq invaded Kuwait. Saudi forces fought alongside troops from the United States, Great Britain, and other countries to drive the invaders out in February 1991. Here Saudi air force jets patrol the desert during the war.

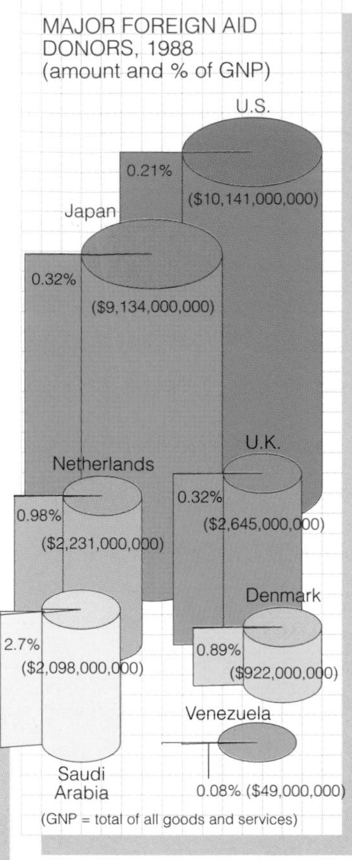

DEFENSE SPENDING, 1992 ($ per head of population)

Country	$ per head
Brazil	9
India	9
China	19
Pakistan	27
Argentina	43
Japan	136
U.K.	366
France	385
U.S.	964
Saudi Arabia	1,371

KEY FACTS

- Saudi Arabia is one of the few countries in the world named after a family.
- Non-Muslims are barred from the holy cities of Mecca and Medina.
- Slavery in Saudi Arabia was abolished in 1961.
- Trading in drugs can result in the death penalty.

Farming in Saudi Arabia used to be limited by lack of water and fertile soil. In the southwest, where the climate is best suited to growing crops, the steep hillsides were terraced to make fields for wheat, coffee, and other produce. In the arid north and east, only the areas around oases could be cultivated. Some villages still use ancient IRRIGATION systems, with modern improvements like electric water pumps.

Since the mid-1980s, farming has developed fast. In 1991 about 4.5 million acres (1.8 million ha) of land were cultivated, nearly twice the area in 1986.

On small farms, vegetables, dates, and other fruit remain the chief crops. Large

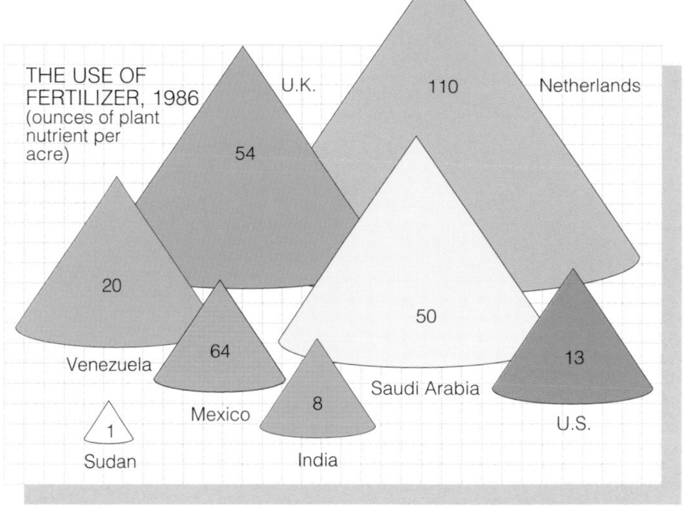

Water for irrigation comes from fossil water and coastal desalination plants. These fields are circular so that a rotating sprinkler can reach the whole area.

◀ ***Fishing in coastal waters provides half the country's needs. Oil pollution in the Persian Gulf in 1991 reduced the local shrimp catch to 1 percent of the level before the Gulf War and destroyed exports to Japan and the United States.***

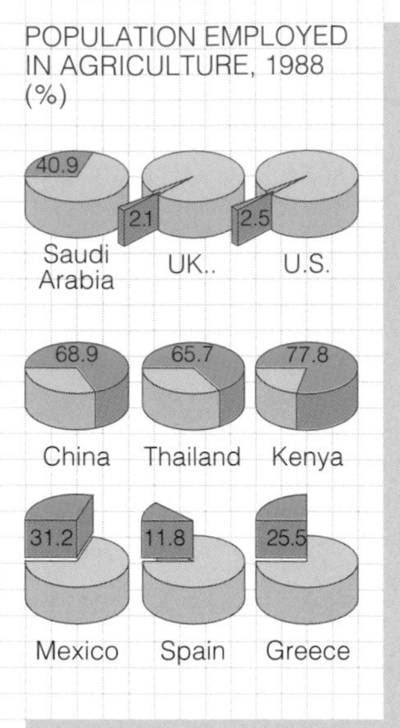

farms use techniques that include precisely controlled irrigation systems, pesticides, chemical fertilizers, drought- and disease-resistant crops, and new cultivation methods, such as HYDROPONICS. This has brought dramatic results: the wheat harvest increased from 142,000 tons in 1979–80 to 3.9 million tons in 1990–91. That year 1.7 million tons were exported. Other crops whose yields have increased are barley, corn, and ALFALFA, which are used for fodder.

The biggest farming projects are in Eastern Province, around the ancient oases of Al-Hufuf and Al-Qatif, and north of Riyadh. By planting TAMARISK trees and grasses to stop the soil from blowing away, thousands of acres of farmland have been reclaimed from the desert. Farmers receive large subsidies from the government, including free water, cheap electricity, and tax benefits. The government buys home-grown wheat at six times the price on world markets.

Saudi Arabia produces all its own dairy products. Dairy cattle are raised intensively near Riyadh. The biggest poultry farm in the Middle East is in Eastern Province.

KEY FACTS

- Saudi Arabia has 12 million date palms. Twenty-nine percent of the annual 500,000-ton date harvest comes from the Riyadh area.
- Saudi Arabia is the world's biggest buyer of live sheep (about 6 million in 1991).
- The country is the sixth biggest exporter of wheat (after the United States, Canada, the EC, Australia, and Argentina).
- Saudi Arabia is the biggest consumer of broiler chickens in the world — 88.2 pounds (40 kg) per person per year.

Dates have been grown in Arabia for 4,000 years. The date palm needs less water than any other crop. A tree can produce fruit for up to 200 years and can yield up to 220 pounds (100 kg) of dates a year.

Breaking the daily fast during Ramadan after sunset with a traditional meal. The women of the household eat separately.

The country still imports much food, including processed food from the United States and Europe, which is popular mainly with expatriates. American-style fast food and international restaurants are available in the cities, but traditional food remains the Saudi favorite.

A celebration feast includes rice with nuts and raisins, *houmus* (a paste made from chick-peas), pita bread, and *tabullah* salad (made with cracked wheat, mint, and parsley). The main dish is a whole roasted lamb. People often eat with their fingers, sharing dishes. Dates and sweet tea are popular snacks.

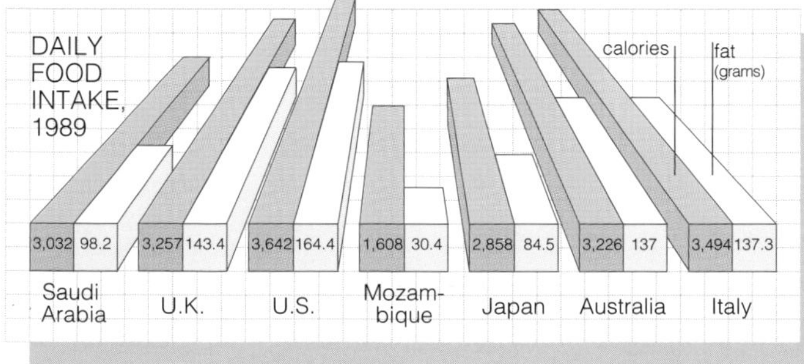

TRADE AND INDUSTRY

THE OIL INDUSTRY

The Saudi economy is based almost totally on producing crude oil and refining it into different products. Some of these are fuels, like petroleum and kerosene. Others (petrochemicals) are raw materials for industry.

Oil was first discovered in Saudi Arabia in the 1930s by American oil companies, who were allowed to produce it in exchange for giving a percentage of their earnings to the government. In the 1960s and 1970s, most oil came from Arab countries. They forced the price up so that foreign oil companies would make better agreements with them. However, in the 1980s new sources (like Alaska and the North Sea) came into production, and the price dropped. Today, oil prices are fairly stable.

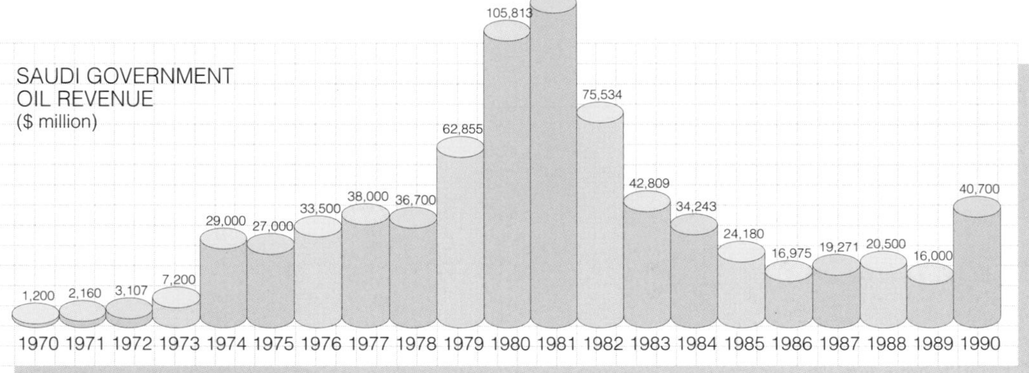

▼ ***The Saudi petrochemicals industry processes oil and gas to make chemicals used in everyday products such as plastics and fertilizer.***

Saudi Aramco is now responsible for all oil production in Saudi Arabia. Its headquarters are at Dhahran. The country's seven oil refineries are at Ras Tannurah and Al-Jubayl on the Persian Gulf, Yanbu' al-Bahr (two refineries), Jeddah and Rabigh on the Red Sea, and Riyadh.

DEVELOPMENT

The Saudi government has used the billions of dollars it has earned from oil to modernize the country's facilities and services by building roads, airports, hospitals, schools, housing, water supplies, and telecommunications services. Since the late 1970s, it has even built two new industrial cities: Al-Jubayl on the gulf coast and Yanbu' al-Bahr on the Red Sea coast, with populations planned to reach 100,000 by the year 2000.

The government has drawn up a series of

◀ ***Crude and refined oil products are exported from Ras Tannurah, where a refinery processes 520,000 barrels of oil a day.***

KEY FACTS

- Oil cost $3 a barrel in 1973, $30 in 1981, and $16 in 1993.
- By 2000, Saudi Arabia will be able to refine 50% of its oil production.
- All companies in the country must be owned mainly by the government or Saudi nationals.
- Saudi Arabia imports all its aviation fuel.
- Industrial exports (apart from oil and gas, fertilizers and petrochemicals) increased by 15% in 1992.
- Saudi Arabia's biggest trading partners are the United States, Great Britain, and Japan for imports, and the United States, Singapore, and France for exports.

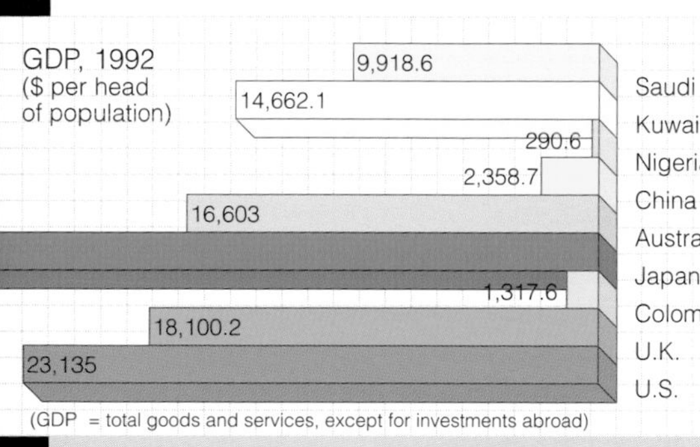

▼ ***The Red Sea fishing port of Yanbu' al Bahr is developing into a major new industrial city.***

plans for development and has set up organizations to coordinate different projects. For example, Saudi Basic Industries Corporation plans and invests in petrochemical companies that process natural gas. It employs 10,000 people in Saudi Arabia and overseas. One of its latest projects is to build a polyester fiber plant at Yanbu' al-Bahr to supply the carpet and bottling industries.

Since oil prices have dropped, Saudi Arabia has made barter deals where it pays for goods and services with oil instead of money. Other trade deals make overseas companies reinvest part of their profits in Saudi Arabia, or provide technical

More Saudi nationals are replacing foreign staff in professional and technical jobs.

The business district in central Riyadh. Banking and insurance are important services. Women have separate banking facilities.

assistance. For example, recently a French company that wanted a defense contract agreed to help a local company establish a gold-refining plant.

OTHER INDUSTRIES

Apart from oil, other industries are centered on the ports of Jeddah, Al-Qatif, and Ad-Dammam, as well as Riyadh. Major products are metals, construction materials, like cement, and food products, such as vegetable oil and milk powder.

Another very important industry is the desalination of seawater, for both irrigation and domestic use. There are 15 desalination plants, which produce 500 million gallons of water a day — 70 percent of the country's needs. Capacity will be doubled by the year 2000. These plants also generate 20 percent of Saudi Arabia's electric power.

TRANSPORTATION

◀ *For centuries, camels (called "the ships of the desert") provided transportation for Arabs and their goods. Now four-wheel-drive vehicles do their job.*

▼ *Two-thirds of hajj pilgrims arrive by air, at a rate of a flight a minute at the busiest time of year. This transit area at Jeddah's King Abdul-Aziz Airport can shelter up to 600,000 people.*

Travel in Saudi Arabia has changed dramatically in recent years. Many families now have more than one car, and there are over 2 million cars in the kingdom. Driving is sometimes chaotic, and more than 20,000 people are killed on the roads each year. Women are not allowed to drive. They usually travel with a private driver or by taxi. Bus services link Saudi towns and neighboring states but are used mainly by migrant workers. There are plans to build a light railroad in the Mecca area, to make travel easier for pilgrims. A 560-mile (900-km) railroad linking the gulf ports and Riyadh is used mainly for freight.

Since 1980, new international airports have been built in Jeddah, Riyadh, Dhahran,

and ad-Dammam. Saudia, the national airline, has a fleet of 111 aircraft and carried 11.5 million passengers on domestic and international routes in 1992.

Oil and gas are pumped from the wellhead to the loading terminal or refinery through a network of pipelines. The giant new 750-mile (1,200-km) Petroline pumps 5 million barrels of oil and gas a day from Al-Jubayl on the east coast to Yanbu' al-Bahr on the west coast. This saves tankers from having to travel around the Arabian coast before going on to Europe or the United States. The pipeline cuts 2,195 miles (3,500 km) off the journey. By 1995, Saudi Arabia was to have 25 supertankers.

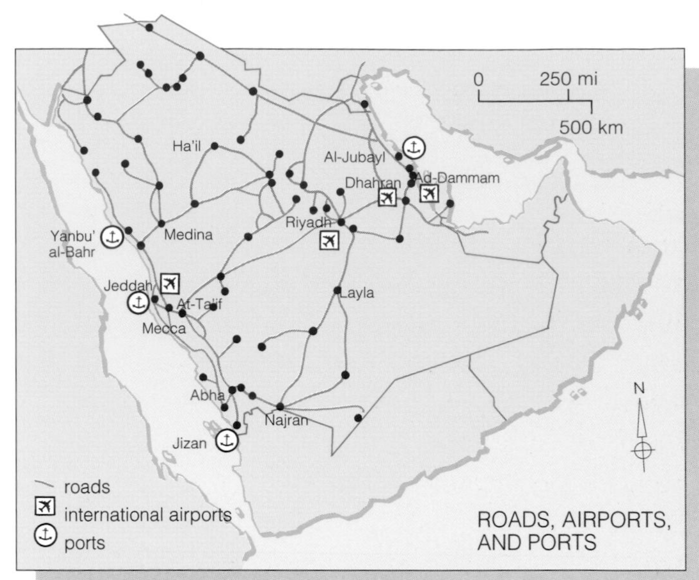

▲ ***There are 76,000 miles (122,000 km) of modern roads in Saudi Arabia.***

▼ ***Saudis rely on private cars and taxis for transportation in the modern city centers.***

KEY FACTS

- Petroleum in Saudi Arabia is the cheapest in the world — about $0.10 a gallon.
- Riyadh has the highest average urban traffic speed in the world — 30 miles per hour (43 kph).
- King Khaled International Airport in Riyadh is the biggest airport in the world — 65 square miles (185 sq km).
- There are about 300,000 private drivers in Saudi Arabia.

THE ENVIRONMENT

The desert is harsh for human life, but many animals, birds, and plants have adapted to its conditions. For example, the camel has a unique ability to survive in the desert. It can walk quickly, 5–9.5 miles per hour (8–16 kph), using little energy, and can live for 10 or 15 days at temperatures of 86–90°F (30–35°C) without drinking. But then it will take in 26 gallons (100 l) of water at one time! Camels also eat thorn bushes and other unappetizing vegetation. Even their eyes have special protection against the frequent blinding sandstorms.

Other mammals in Saudi Arabia include many types of gazelles and members of the cat family — from mountain leopards to tiny sand cats (ancestors of our domestic tabbies). There are baboons, wolves, foxes, and mongooses, too. Reptiles include scorpions, lizards, and snakes, such as cobras, sidewinders, and vipers. Locusts (migrating from East Africa) and mosquitos used to be a problem, but today their numbers have been limited by pesticides.

In the early part of the 20th century, hunting with automatic rifles was a popular activity. This severely reduced the numbers of game animals in Saudi Arabia, and some became extinct. Now only two traditional kinds of hunting are allowed: falconry and COURSING with the Arabian hunting dog, the saluki.

The country's coastal waters and islands

In 1991 the shallow tidal zone of the Persian Gulf was polluted by sticky black crude oil. Damage still continues.

are home to many different creatures. Giant moray eels and manta rays live in the Red Sea. A manta ray can have a wingspan of 16 feet (5 m) and weigh several tons. Stonefish have poisonous spines, and lionfish sting. DUGONGS, whales, and dolphins are found in the Persian Gulf as well as the Red Sea. The shallow coastal waters of the Persian Gulf also contain oyster beds, whose pearls are among the best in the world. They have been harvested for thousands of years. About 90 percent of Saudi Arabia's turtles breed on the offshore coral islands.

The greatest risk of pollution in Saudi Arabia is from accidental oil spillages. The equivalent of 250,000 barrels of oil are spilled into the Persian Gulf each year. Burning off gas at oil wellheads releases carbon dioxide into the atmosphere. However, because Saudi crude oil has a relatively low sulfur content, and there is little rainfall, there is less risk of acid rain.

During the Gulf War in 1991, when oil storage tanks on the coast of Kuwait exploded, there was a near catastrophe. About 3 to 4 million barrels of oil were

KEY FACTS

- Over 6 billion migrating birds fly over or visit Saudi Arabia each year.
- The rare rheem gazelle may spend its whole life without drinking water. It finds moisture in plants and by licking dew off its coat.
- The "desert shrimp" grows, mates, and dies within a few days in the pools left after rainstorms. The eggs lie dormant for up to 20 years for the next rain before hatching.
- Sea snakes in the Persian Gulf are among the world's deadliest. One drop of their venom could kill five adults.
- The camel was domesticated in Arabia 4,000 years ago and the saluki 8,000 years ago.
- With Saudi help, the native Arabian oryx was reintroduced into the wild in 1980. Before then, it had survived only in captivity.

The Arabian mountain leopard, one of sixteen endangered native mammals. Lions disappeared in the middle of the 19th century, ostriches became extinct in the 1930s, and the last wild cheetah was shot in 1973.

Falconry requires great skill. Falconers train young hawks to fly free to attack their prey and then return to the falconer's wrist.

released into the ocean, and the slick spread 267 miles (430 km) southeast along the Saudi coast as far as ad-Dammam. Half the oil evaporated, the equivalent of 300,000 barrels was recovered, and the rest sank down to the seabed. About 20,000 seabirds died, while unknown numbers of fish and other marine life were destroyed or contaminated. The long-term effects on marine life are still not certain. One positive result was that rescuers cleared garbage from the offshore coral islands, and now their turtle populations have increased.

Groundwater accumulated over thousands of years has been heavily used for irrigation and drinking water in the eastern region. This has reduced supplies in some places. A new danger is the heavy use of fertilizers, which can contaminate the groundwater. The soil can also be ruined by excessive watering, which forms a crust of mineral salts on the surface. But one positive effect of increased watering has been more bird life, especially in the east. Birds migrating for the winter, from Central Asia to Africa and from northern Europe to India, take a break from their long journeys in Saudi Arabia. The number of bird species found at pools of treated sewage water in al-Hair reserve, south of Riyadh, has

The northern Red Sea contains some spectacular coral gardens. Special conditions make it easier for the 177 coral species to grow at some of the fastest rates recorded, up to 15 inches (39 cm) a year.

A modern shopping mall contrasting with the natural environment, cool and shaded from the glaring sun, depends on electric power for light, air-conditioning, and an escalator.

increased from 90 to 270 in 10 years.

Since the 1980s, the government has been encouraging conservation. By 1995, there should be 56 wildlife reserves and 52 marine area reserves throughout the country. The most important reserve is the mountainous National Park of the Asir, covering 1,738 square miles (4,500 sq km). This region is the richest in wildlife. It also contains remote areas of special interest. Above the 6,000-foot (1,800-m) line, juniper forests and other plants match the plant life of northern Greece, thousands of miles away. They are survivors from the region's cooler climate during the last Ice Age. Tourism is growing in all these areas.

Riyadh Zoo, created in 1987, is world-class. It houses 1,400 animals of 350 different species. These include some endangered native creatures, such as the houbara bustard, the griffon vulture, and the sand cat. Also, brown bears and ostriches, which are extinct in the wild in Saudi Arabia, can be found at the zoo. The zoo also conserves rare species like the Arabian leopard, the cheetah, and the bataleur eagle.

Environmental awareness in Saudi Arabia has been slow to increase. Lead-free petroleum will be available in 1995, but household waste materials are not recycled. Garbage is collected under contract to overseas companies. The work is done by foreign laborers.

THE FUTURE

Within three generations Saudi Arabia has been transformed. Its huge oil wealth has been used to create modern services to which all its people have free access. Many Saudi families today enjoy a luxurious standard of living.

This rapid change has only been possible by hiring foreign experts and laborers to work in the country and by importing all the necessary equipment and high technology. The only income Saudi Arabia has to pay for all this comes from selling oil.

In recent years the price of oil has fallen to about half of its peak price in 1981. The price is not likely to rise to such a high level again. New sources of oil and gas, for example, in Siberia and Vietnam, will become easily available to the industrialized countries that buy the most fuel. If Saudi Arabia's income falls, its development plans will have to become more modest.

Because the Middle East has been the scene of many political and religious disputes, Saudi Arabia (like other oil producers in the region) has had to build strong defense forces. Its export routes pass through the Persian Gulf and the Red Sea, which are both vulnerable areas. Already Saudi Arabia spends about a third of its budget on military equipment and armed forces. Iraq's invasion of Kuwait in 1990 is a reminder of the dangers in the region.

If government spending has to drop, certain social changes will speed up. The country's strict rules of behavior are being challenged more and more. Already, educated Saudis are filling more jobs previously held by expatriates. Educated

KEY FACTS

- In 1989 over 400 people died when the Great Mosque at Mecca was besieged by Iranians who demanded control of the holy places.
- In 1990, 42 Saudi women protesters drove around Riyadh illegally for about half an hour before they were arrested. They were soon released.
- In 1985 Prince Sultan Ibn Sulman became the first Arab, the first Muslim, and the first member of royalty to go on a space mission.

Some qualified Saudi women have jobs. In the future they will ask for more choice and recognition in their careers.

women especially are beginning to want to enter careers that they have been trained for. Many Saudis have traveled overseas, have seen foreign movies, and now have satellite television, so they are encountering new ideas and different ways of living.

The future of Saudi Arabia may also change when the Arab countries reach a final peace with Israel. The first steps toward this were taken in September 1993. If there is a lasting peace, there will be new opportunities for development. Perhaps the old pipeline for exporting Saudi oil from the Mediterranean will reopen, and there will be prosperous trade between countries in the region.

One danger is that the old enemy Israel will be replaced by new threats. For example, extreme Muslim groups in Iran have made it clear they want to control the holy places in Saudi Arabia.

Although Saudi oil reserves will last for 100 years, or about five generations, at the present rate of production, it is not easy to know whether or not the future will be peaceful and prosperous. The answer depends partly on people in the rest of the world. Will we continue to use oil and gas at the same ever-increasing rate that we do now?

Pipelines pump oil and gas across scorching sandy wastes. The deserts of Saudi Arabia will remain long after its underground resources run out.

A NOTE ON ISLAM

Islam was founded in the land that is now Saudi Arabia in the 7th century. Muslims believe that the Prophet Muhammad received God's message from the Angel Gabriel and that he was the last in a line of prophets which started with Adam and included Abraham, Moses, and Jesus.

Muhammad was born in about A.D. 570. He despised the corruption of Mecca and the worship of many different gods that was practiced there. When he was about 40 years old, he received his first revelation (message from God), but, when he began to preach in Mecca, he was persecuted. He and his followers then fled to Medina, where he was well received. In 630 he returned to Mecca, but died two years later. Muhammad's revelation was later recorded in the Muslims' holy book, the Koran, which has 114 chapters and 6,263 verses. It is written in Arabic.

Islam means "submission," and Muslims believe it is a duty to submit to the will of Allah, the One True God. Religious duties and rules of behavior are laid down in the Koran and in the *Hadith* (the sayings and deeds of Muhammad). Behavior that is forbidden includes gambling and eating certain "unclean" foods.

The central beliefs are called the Five Pillars of Islam. They are:

1. To profess the faith ("There is no god but God, and Muhammad is the Messenger of God").
2. Prayer (Arabic, *salat*). There are no priests in Islam, because every Muslim speaks directly to God.
3. Charity (Arabic, *zakat*). All things belong to God, but wealth is purified by giving to those who are in need.
4. Fasting (Arabic, *sawn*). During the month of Ramadan, Muslims fast from sunrise to sunset, without even drinking water.
5. Pilgrimage (Arabic, *hajj*). All Muslims are required to make the holy journey to Mecca once in their lives, if they can afford it and are well enough.

FURTHER INFORMATION

- AMERICAN/SAUDI BUSINESS ROUND TABLE
25 Smith Street, Suite 301, Nanuet, NY 10954
- ISLAMIC INFORMATION CENTER OF AMERICA
Box 4052, Des Plaines, IL 60016
- ROYAL EMBASSY OF SAUDI ARABIA
601 New Hampshire Avenue N.W., Washington, D.C. 20037

BOOKS ABOUT SAUDI ARABIA

Deegan, Paul J. *Persian Gulf Nations.* Abdo and Daughters, 1991

Foster, Leila M. *Saudi Arabia*. Childrens, 1993

Morrison, Ian A. *Middle East*. Raintree Steck-Vaughn, 1991

Steins, Richard. *The Mideast after the Gulf War.* Millbrook, 1992

GLOSSARY

ALFALFA
A crop grown for animal feed

COURSING
Using trained dogs to hunt and catch prey

DESALINATION
A process that takes the salt out of seawater to make it fit to drink or to water crops

DUGONG
A large marine mammal, also known as the sea cow, which lives on vegetation alone

EXPATRIATE
A foreigner who is living in another country to work

FOSSIL WATER
Water that fell as rain centuries ago and is stored in natural reservoirs underground

HAJJ
The Muslim pilgrimage to Mecca

HYDROPONICS
Growing plants without soil, in water enriched with chemical nutrients

IMAM
A Muslim religious leader

IRRIGATION
Artificial water supply for cultivating crops, for example using water channels and mechanized sprinklers

KORAN
The holy book of Islam

MADRASSA
A Muslim school where children are instructed in the Koran

MAJLIS
A meeting where the king or tribal leader hears complaints and settles disputes

MANGROVE
A tree that can live in salt water and grows in muddy tidal swamps in the tropics

MONSOON
Seasonal rains

MOSQUE
Muslim place of worship

MUEZZIN
The man who calls the Muslim faithful to prayer at a mosque

MUTAWA
The religious police in Saudi Arabia, who enforce rules of behavior

NOMADS
People who move from place to place with their livestock to take advantage of seasonal grazing and water supplies

PENINSULA
Area of land with water on three sides

PILGRIMAGE
A journey to worship at a holy shrine

QADI
A religious judge at a *sharia* court

SHAMAL
A cold and dusty northwesterly wind of Arabia

SHARIA
The Islamic system of law

SOUK
A bazaar or market, often a series of covered alleys, with special areas for the sale of different goods, such as gold or spices

TAMARISK
A salt- and drought-resistant tree, adapted to desert conditions

TERRACES
Fields that are built by leveling sections of hillsides

WADI
A seasonal riverbed

INDEX

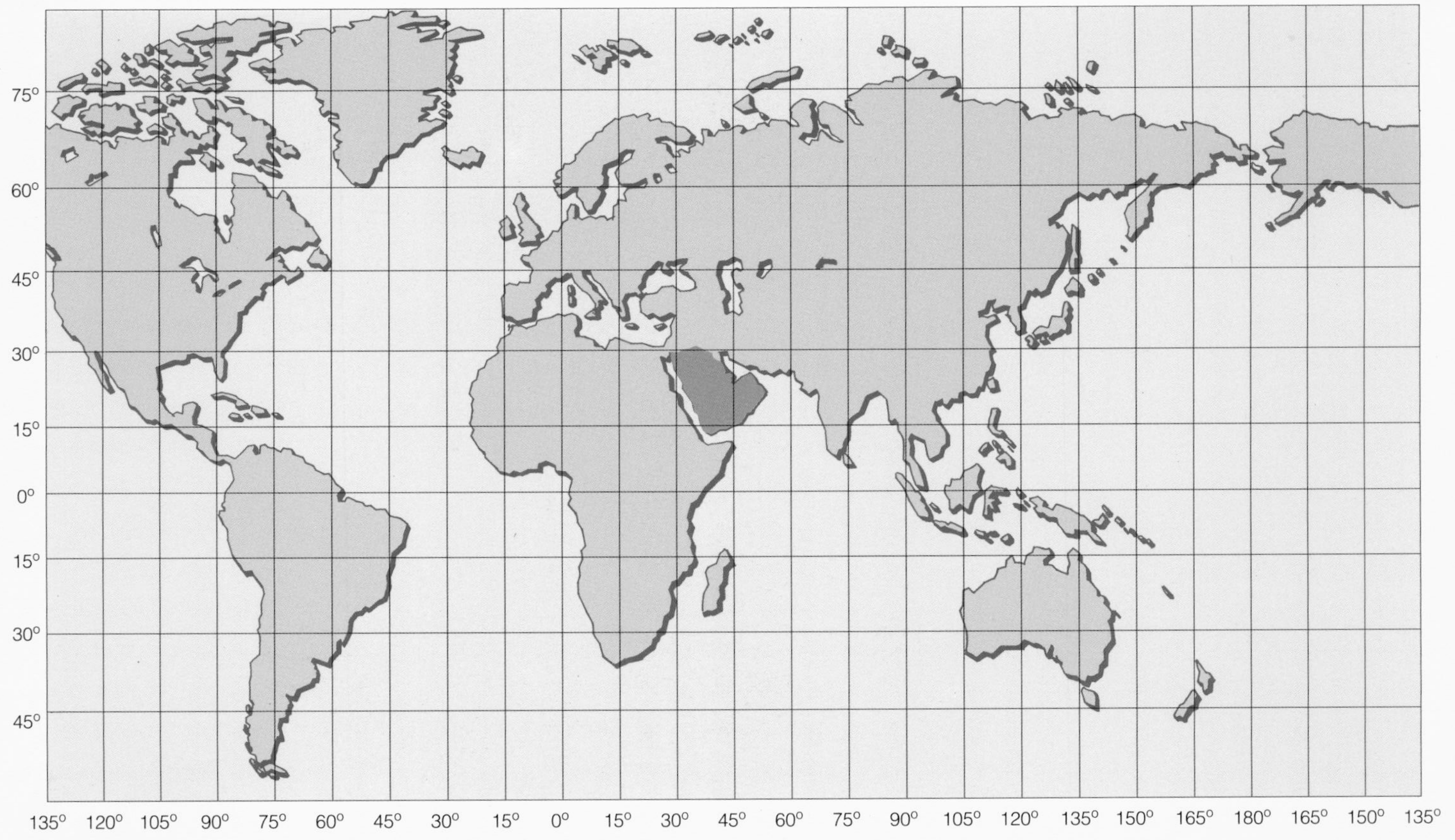
75°
60°
45°
30°
15°
0°
15°
30°
45°
135° 120° 105° 90° 75° 60° 45° 30° 15° 0° 15° 30° 45° 60° 75° 90° 105° 120° 135° 150° 165° 180° 165° 150° 135°

IRAQ
IRAN
JORDAN
KUWAIT
PERSIAN GULF
EGYPT
RED SEA
SAUDI ARABIA
RIYADH
Tabuk
Ha'il
Buraydah
Medina
Yanbu' al-Bahr
Rabigh
Jeddah
Mecca
At-Ta'if
Abha
Najran
Jizan
Layla
Al-Jubayl
Ras Tannurah
Al-Qatif
Ad-Dammam
Dhahran
Al-Hufuf
BAHRAIN
QATAR
UNITED ARAB EMIRATES
STRAIT OF HORMUZ
OMAN
GULF OF OMAN
Tropic of Cancer
20°
20°
SUDAN
ERITREA
ETHIOPIA
DJIBOUTI
BAB EL MANDEB STRAITS
FARASAN ISLANDS
YEMEN
GULF OF ADEN
ARABIAN SEA
N
S
E
W
0
250 mi
500 km